GW00372267

PRAISE FOR *KEEPING BEES*

'Occasionally naked yet always well-turned-out, some of these poems call to mind the spiritual-erotic quality of early Leonard Cohen, though the voice is unmistakably Dimitra Xidous' own. Brimful of soul, and beautifully written, *Keeping Bees* is one of the most impressive and expressive poetry debuts in a long time.'

— Patrick Chapman
Author of *A Promiscuity of Spines* (Salmon Poetry)
and *The Negative Cutter* (Arlen House)

'"he says I have a very sexual view of love..."

... and she does, Dimitra Xidous is a truly delicious writer. She feasts upon the body in *Keeping Bees*. A strong unique voice; at times a young Aristotle and that obsession with natural process, at times her tones are of the sharp artist palette of Bishop, but more often laced with a sensual evocation of a female Neruda. This voice is as strong and unique as any young poet writing in English today. I was left breathless. Astounding originality, Xidous is fearless.'

— Elaine Feeney
Author of *The Radio Was Gospel* (Salmon Poetry)

'Honest, refreshing, daring, at times even arousing. A collection centered on the subject of instinct and on the instinctual subject. Poems by a wide-eyed mind about the body and all of its thrills. Poems that push at the limits of respectability and solitude until those limits dissolve. Poems then of true presence, real impact that will affect you in the gut, in the plexus, in the glands, the cortices, the nerves. And so one I'll be taking down often from my shelf by the bed from now on.'

— Dave Lordan
Author of *Invitation to a Sacrifice* (Salmon Poetry)
and *First Book of Frags* (Wurm Press)

KEEPING BEES

KEEPING BEES

Dimitra Xidous

Doire Press

First published in March 2014

Doire Press
Aille, Inverin
Co. Galway
www.doirepress.com

Layout & cover design: Lisa Frank
Cover artwork: Ria Czerniak
Author photo: Aidan Murphy

Printed by Clódóirí CL
Casla, Co. na Gaillimhe

Copyright © Dimitra Xidous

ISBN 978-1-907682-32-2

All rights reserved. No part of this publication may be reproduced or transmitted in any form or by any means. This book is sold subject to the usual trade conditions.

ACKNOWLEDGEMENTS

Acknowledgements are due to the editors of the following publications in which versions of some of these poems first appeared: *The Bare Hands Anthology, Bare Hands Poetry, The Bohemyth, Burning Bush II, Bywords, Bywords Quarterly Journal, Colony, Room, The Penny Dreadful, The Stinging Fly, The Weary Blues and Wordlegs.*

'Holes' was a finalist in the 2014 *Malahat Review* Open Season Awards and 'Keeping Bees' was shortlisted for the 2013 Bridport Poetry Prize.

I wish to thank the following people for their ongoing support and encouragement: Sandra Black, Laura Canning, Patrick Chapman, Amanda Earl, Elaine Feeney, Anna Gruending, Luke Jones, Marita Killen, Dave Lordan, Aidan Murphy, Stephen Murray, Kerrie O'Brien, Sharon Peake, Elizabeth Reapy, Nick Seymour, Ronan Sheehan, Natalie St Lawrence, Anne Tannam, Casey Tosh, my parents Joanna and Michael, and my sisters, Asimina and Maria.

Further thanks to Julia Schipper and Lucero Hernandez — two of life's soulmates — and to Ria Czerniak for making visual art of the words. And finally, to Janice Kulyk Keefer, in whose poetry class I first heard the word *duende* uttered, and my whole body shook.

CONTENTS

Easter   13

Onions   14

Animals   15

Raisins   16

Hung   17

Here is a Box (Vive La Petite Mort!)   18

Dogs Panting   22

Hello Dalí   23

With a Lemon for a Tongue That Girl Will Never Love Anyone   24

In the Shower You Told Me You Like Christmas   25

You Cannot Tell Me   26

The Body, Heart and Thumb   27

Six Pack   29

Bone Collector   30

Without Ceremony   31

Chicken Feet   32

The Science of Hands   33

Death is Always Inevitable   34

Peach Season   35

Keeping Bees   37

Fig   38

Vinegar   40

The Body of Christ   41

Like Oranges   43

Love is Stuck   45

In Defence of Lemons   46

Honey   47

I Do Not Think My Eyes are Pretty   48

Sweet Morag   49

Horse Logic   50

Bee's Wing   51

The New Woman   52

Holes   53

Ovum   55

You Taste of Fish   56

Salt   57

Goya Knew Better   59

Your Hand Does Not Impress Me as Much   60

Maggot Fingers   61

Flies   62

Madrid is a Woman   64

Love Bares the Wood   65

The Bees   66

About the Author   68

About the Artist   69

Notes   70

To burn with desire and keep quiet about it is the greatest punishment we can bring on ourselves.

— Frederico García Lorca, *Blood Wedding and Yerma*

Easter

Here is vinegar and passion,
poison and sadness

and the sound of a clarinet
and a room with a sink;
here is a butcher with a knife
and a nail through the wrist;

here, a hot oven
and a machine that measures weights;
and here is a table, and a high mount:

here is a lamb
and slices of a sin
and pieces of a body
and meat between thieves.

Onions

My grandmother picked tomatoes that looked pregnant
because she said they made the best salads.

Sitting in her kitchen I'd watch her knife away,
separating cucumbers from prophylactic skins.
In all her years she had gathered a wisdom
the citizens of burnt-down Troy would envy.

Her hands shook with widowhood and old age
but she never let it slip — the knife was now a heavy part
taking the place of a uterus which used to grow
into all kinds of nutritious sizes. The first real intimacy
I spied, lived in those raw cucumbers as she let water
lick them in corners most exposed.

Always, the onions were left to the end.
It has taken years but finally, I understand that
breaking down an onion is nothing short of murder.
Like a surgeon ill-taught in the proper ways
to excavate the human body, my grandmother grew
merciless with the onions because they were merciless with her.

She could never cry for the dead the way she cried with them.

Animals

You loved a man with more hands than a parade of beggars.
— Marty McConnell, from 'Frida Kahlo to Marty McConnell'

Maybe I was a beggar.
Then again, how can I
be sure when lovers and
beggars look the same.
It is easier to believe
I was an animal instead;
I've seen animals do
the things I did with you.

Raisins

Once upon a time full
and hanging, now gone
infertile, never to make
wine —

they cave in, become
narcissistic and love
to touch themselves.

Beyond the plump,
they will not bounce
back — not like toes
and fingers after being left
too long in the bath;

instead, like women longing
to cradle milk and sex in cells
that have forgotten how to be
breasts, they have fallen out of
grace with God.

Dried to this end by a sun
that began its murdering ways
in the days of Icarus, they are
forever clenched in ecstasy
like a dead man hanging by
a noose.

Hung

Whenever anyone asked him about the symbolism
he'd answer *'a bull is a bull and a horse is a horse'*
and really, he's right about that. Still, it was there,
in the horse most of all — a spear through the body,
throat tight, mouth like a vulva ajar choking on the meat
of an intruder — yes, it was there, in the horse most of all
where Picasso got it right, the way a living thing will react
to an attack on the body: he knew to paint it open;
agony exists best in the open, and sometimes also,
where there is a hole.

Leading up to *Guernica*, he practiced by painting
a horse with a beautiful body — healthy, plump, and
strong as any woman's before she knows to fear
the sounds of guns, bombs, and unwanted sex. Next to it,
he painted a figure, thin as a stem, hung like a boy.

Here is a Box (Vive La Petite Mort!)

1

Here is a box. You cannot tick it,
flick it or lick it. It is not that kind of box.
You cannot get sick in it, toss a stick in it
or put your dick in it. It is not that kind of box.
You cannot tickle it, pickle it or be fickle with it.
It is not that kind of box.

It is not the kind of box to sleep in, weep in
or reap what you sow in. This is the kind of box
that is good for turning one thing into another.
It is the kind of box to go deep in.

2

Someone once told me I had a small box,
too small for any man to fit, which made me
think of grapes: little boxes growing in clusters

each cluster dangling like a tit
off the vine, each cluster going sour
for being beyond a fox's reach.

Sometimes, I wonder if he lulls himself to sleep
thinking only death will succeed,
for going sour already puts me within reach.

But death is not about going sour, it just turns
one thing into another. Death makes it possible
to pour wine from a box; *la petite mort*
makes it taste good.

3

Here is a box. You cannot pluck it,
suck it or spelunk it. It is not that kind of box.
You cannot draw a map on it, put your stamp on it
or tap that ass with it. It is not that kind of box.
You cannot sink it, drink it or be surrounded by the pink of it.
It is not that kind of box.

It is not the kind of box to be a hound in, make a sound in
or lay around in. This is the kind of box
that is good for turning one thing into another.
It is the kind of box to go down in.

4

Someone once told me I had a sexual view of love,
too sexual for it to be love at all, but a box is full of room
and a room can be full of box provided there is at least
one woman standing in it. And sometimes, all it takes is one.

I used to have a necklace and I would run it down
the length of my body just so I could watch it slide over my hips
because it was one way to measure the full weight of love.
The only other way takes up much less space:
the shenanigans of intimacy boil down to what
passes between two people when their mouths are open
and desire hangs like a dog's tongue. Here, love is the pits
of two cherries so long as you can get through the flesh.
For all the times that I cannot, I wish I had that necklace
but that necklace has been lost.

And death is not about loss, it just turns
one thing into another. Death gnaws at the flesh
to find love in the pits, but it is *la petite mort*
that makes love bearable.

5

Here is a box. You cannot fling it,
sting it or put a ring on it. It is not that kind of box.
You cannot bag it, tag it or put a fag out on it. It is not
that kind of box. You cannot be a god in it, put your rod
in it or stuff a cod in it. It is not that kind of box.

It is not the kind of box to be rough in, crave a muff in
or do as the doctor says and turn and cough in. This is the kind of box
that is good for turning one thing into another.
It is the kind of box to go off in.

6

Cemeteries are full of boxes
turning one thing into another —
cemeteries are like wombs this way.

The body comes raging out of a box
this is how the body starts —
the end result of juice and flesh

turning one thing into another
all the rage of two raging lovers
who cannot smell their own slow decay

because that is how it is, from the moment we start.
From the moment we start
decay does not rage in the same way.

But death is not about decay, it just turns
one thing into another. Death puts us into
one kind of box but it is *la petite mort*
that pulls us out of our mothers.

7

Here is a box. Somewhere there is another kind of box
and it is having more fun than this box. Whatever
gnaws at us — from the moment we start — this is
the kind of box that knows the bones are for the dogs.

So go on and lay yourself down —
this is the kind of box to snog in, jam your log in
and be a dog in.

Dogs Panting

He showed up
at the hotel
in running shoes

and I remembered
the time, while riding
the metro in Madrid,

I saw two boys
sitting together —
their shoes

with laces undone
were like four dogs
panting

I would fuck her
I would fuck her
I would fuck her

until they got off
at Tirso de Molina,
and I didn't.

I've since come to take it
as a sign of a man
who wants to get it on.

A man who wants to get it on
will always show up in shoes
that have their own tongues.

Hello Dalí

Surrealism is destructive, but it destroys only what it considers to be shackles limiting our vision.

— Salvador Dalí

I want to talk to Dalí about his painting
tell him he paints a good egg
that it has the shape of all the eggs
and even though I wouldn't hate him
if he told me he sucked the yolk
into his brush because he wanted to keep
the nutritious yellow for something else,
I want to tell him I am concerned about
those bodies — hers and the one tearing
through the shell. I want to tell him
not all peckers are created equal and as far as
what came first, it is clear the body
tearing through the shell is not the father
of the child between her legs, that as far as
bodies go, something more like a chicken
would have been better. She looks like
she could use some food.

With a Lemon for a Tongue That Girl Will Never Love Anyone

With a lemon for a tongue
she burns the house down

or simply singes the hairs
off the legs of lovers

without leaving a mark;
it all depends on the heat in the encounter.

With a lemon for a tongue
she cuts a sharp figure —

the tongue tip, taut
and inviting as a nipple

drips comfort, and all her lovers take her in
and all her lovers say loving her feels like a bee's sting.

With a lemon for a tongue
she glows like sunshine:

a halo of round yellow, a bird's beak
of colour, that small dribble of piss

turning every dark and lush hole
into a sour puss.

With a lemon for a tongue
she spits acid, aims for the eyes

because this is what she thinks it means
when she hears people say *love is blind*.

In the Shower You Told Me You Like Christmas

I never said a thing; the shower wasn't big enough
for you and me, and Jesus. But if Jesus could have fit
in that finite space between us

maybe there, on the nape of your neck
yielding like the lip of a coffee cup, or there
on my back, where you touched me with hands

that were no longer those of a bartender
not yet those of a scientist

I would have told you
I like Easter better.

Looking back fondly, in the shower —
there and elsewhere —

I was the Jesus
who got nailed.

You Cannot Tell Me

We're all curious about what might hurt us.

— Federico García Lorca

after Cormac

You cannot tell me love is a cockroach
      if you haven't seen it run across the floor
or convince me that freedom is a dove
      if you haven't seen it fly past your window.

You cannot tell me sadness is a lamb
      if you haven't seen it hanging in the slaughterhouse
or make me believe that forgiveness is a fish
      if you haven't seen it swim like a ribbon in water.

You cannot tell me what I already know.

Love turns us into insects; we're nothing more than fragile,
crawling on the floor. Sadness hangs after slaughter.
Sadness is a lamb eaten at Easter, and the day after.

But freedom is not a dove; forgiveness, not a fish.
If it were so —

               my lover would have sent me a dove,
               my lover would have given me a fish.

The Body, Heart and Thumb

a severed thumb
so perfect and rough
has started to smell
now the mourners come

they've come to have a look
so perfect and rough
they're curious to see
how dead a thumb can be

death gives each a glance
so perfect and rough
of a beauty that is unique
because death happens to everything only once

yet the mourners ask for more proof
so perfect and rough
they want the rest of the body
the thumb was severed from

•

the rest of the body
the thumb was severed from
was severed from its thumb
because it had to make a choice
between the heart and the thumb
and those doing the collecting
would not be satisfied until
they got their hands on one, or the other

those doing the collecting
are never satisfied
those doing the collecting

believe the body has to make a choice
between the heart and the thumb —
when it comes to love, they say
when love comes undone
oh yes, we will get our hands on one, or the other

when it comes to love, they say
to prove it was really love
when love comes undone
the body must make a sacrifice
between the heart and the thumb
without question, the body must give up one
and like Abraham holding a knife to his son
the body must make a lamb of one, or the other

without question, the body must give up one
and those doing the collecting will tell you
when you have to make the choice
one is better than the other —
between the heart and the thumb
it is better to give up the thumb;
those who choose to get rid of the heart
will have to bare the hole when they hear people say
there goes a body, a body that has not loved

Six Pack

It's the morning after; I watch you
roll up your underwear, your hands moving
like a torcedor. Whatever remained
of your fingers and thumbs inch along
the way caterpillars do, making
                              slow
                                        progress.

I think back to the night before, how your fingers
and thumbs danced like worms in the rain,
how my body shifted under exuberant twitches,
how my mouth lost its lips, became sharp, yellow
and desired you. When you finish, you tell me
these came from a pack of six — and
                              I want you.
                                        Again.

As bones of wings pop through skin
you pray I've lost my appetite for worms, forgetting
birds get off on the taste of caterpillars too.

Bone Collector

Your erection, sweet and heavy,
a scavenger shovelling dirtfuls of fuck
into wet cunts, shakes like a diviner rod
when you get close. Yet, you are not interested
in wet or water; no, you just want your rib back.
You tell me it wasn't His to take, wasn't His to make
another body, leave a hole in the one he made for you.

You should know the rib I've got isn't yours.
The one I've got belonged to a priest because God knew
he'd think his bone was the one that made Mary —
the one who didn't need a boning to fill her up with grace.
But you are not interested in the immaculate or why it made her holy
to lie there then, to get filled up with grace — God knows
asking for consent is a dirty thing; no, all you know is that
it's a desperate hole you don't want anymore.

So what's a girl to do? Yes, what's a girl to do
when you feel so low, so low with your desperate hole?
I've got one tighter than holy, and it's the kind of hole that craves
a good bone, sweet and heavy all the more.

Without Ceremony

Greek coffee turns the cup
into a sort of earth, the kind
for digging graves into —

her tongue breaks the surface
like the word yes, spoken to break
the sound of skin collapsing.

The dirt of grounds
that never settled to the bottom
are not interested in telling her the future —

tasting only of the present
they slide down her throat
like earthworms; it feels like
being buried alive.

Sometime later it will hit her —
bodies that go to dirt
without ceremony

go to dirt
with no stones
to mark their places.

Chicken Feet

we ran after footballs and tore into oranges
with our eyes, fingers, teeth

kicking at empty boxes to prove we had no fear
our exposed bellies were like lions
yawning in the Greek heat

in the yard, my grandmother
had a pot of water on the boil

inside, a chicken sat limp and folded —
head dangling over the side
like a dead hand

there was nothing dead about hers though
and we watched as she went about the business of butchery

pulling first at the feathers then at the insides
the chicken needed no more manicuring
to become food

claws and nails remained
curled in a *rigor mortis* grin

back then
it was easy to picture death smiling
her mouth sharp and yellow.

The Science of Hands

after Lorna Crozier

The science of hands is simple: for the right one, and the left one,
four fingers and a thumb. Hands are the lambs of the body:
vulnerable to slaughter.

There is a story about a woman who lost her hands to a man —
he touched them and made them less than flesh, only to find them
again when another man touched the space where her hands once were;
he brought them back, made them flesh again.

If a lover's hands are shaped like fish, on the one hand,
it could mean something; on the other, it could mean nothing.

Eating with one's hands is better than prayer, though even there,
Christ brought the two together. But before it was his body,
it was just a piece of bread in his hand.

When two languages collide and there is no way of knowing
what is said or understood, it is the hands that speak. Hands speak
love and there is nothing between the legs or on the tip of the tongue
that knows the intimacy of words like the hand-written syllables
of a love letter.

Most of all, they know when the end is coming:
think of all the hands that waved good-bye on the Titanic.

Death is Always Inevitable

This is how death fills the space
between beds and ceilings:

two oxygen tanks
go rigid for being useless; meanwhile,
back in Canada, your granddaughter
opens the book to a scene of
cyanide suicide, the smell of
bitter almonds leaking out
of a dead mouth, and it starts
like this:
                    It was inevitable…
these are Marquez's first words
on the subject, and they float up
from the open mouth of the page;
meanwhile, back in Greece, the last
words are all yours, and they fall
like fruit into the basket

of my father's ear.

Peach Season

for Bob

If the dirt of my body came
straight from the Okanagan Valley
the fat of them would taste of peaches.

Nipples, taut and high as baby birds
stretching out for food, choke
on the excitement of new life and you
touching me for the first time:

the bees of your fingers and thumbs
buzz little circles into my flesh, find something
that feels like a marble rolling under the skin
and I remember

the mammogram, how it turned them both
to fruit leather — flattened, so that the breastedness of them
spread out until they were nothing — and I remember
how it felt. I remember.

I break the silence to tell you
they're fine, I'm fine
but the sting of intimacy
leaves a mark on everything it touches:
I know you know what cancer feels like.

The best peach I ever had came all the way
from British Columbia: a yolkful of fruitedness,
a line creasing down the skin of it,
making cleavage — it was the closest thing
to having something holy in my mouth
and I swear it glowed going down my throat.

It was March when you sent that text
to tell me *I miss your boobs,* and even though
peach season was long gone

I went to Penney's, found a t-shirt with two shells
on the front — one for right there and there, where
the nest of my breasts rests, where the sting
of intimacy left its mark — and I thought

I'll wear it the next time, help you find them again:

two birds cupped in your hands
bring back the taste of peach to your mouth.

Keeping Bees

In the morning, after he's kissed you
(sucked your left nipple so hard it aches)
he says he wants to make his own honey
and you tell him that's what your father did
when he came to Canada in the '70s
(and you wish you could show him a picture
of your dad dressed as a beekeeper
but you live in Dublin now, and all those photos
are back home) and he tells you

he wants to grow his own vegetables
and so you tell him that your parents' garden
is full of them — tomatoes and zucchinis
and long beans — enough of everything for stew
all summer and autumn, and you tell him
your dad comes from the tomato capital of Greece
(and you want to tell him how when you were a little girl
you used to eat them like apples; you want tell him
about the seeds — how they were so much better
than jam — but your nipples are on fire and your breasts
are the bums of two bees in love) and all he says is

there's not enough time, so instead
you ask him how he feels and he says he's haunted
and he holds you and says nothing, and your body
buzzes — your nipples poke his skin, and they love him
and the rest of you loves him too (you want to tell him
that love is equal parts honey and sting, and where love rumbles
bodies sound like beehives) but he doesn't know how he feels
except that he wants to grow vegetables, because the ground
owes him something for what the ground has taken in;
he wants to make his own honey, keep his own bees
and wait for a message from the dead.

Fig

i. What a woman looks like on the inside

I have discovered figs.
I think of a virgin getting ready
for his first woman.

Sitting in my kitchen, becoming
a different kind of cannibal, I bend
my tongue to get fig deep, the way
a boy bends to get to a place where he feels
surrounded and sweet — in the body,
the fruit.

I wonder how big the figs grew in the Garden —
if that's the tree he slept under while the snake
was pulling back the folds in Eve.

ii. He calls my body an umbrella

He likes the way I open
how rigid my bones can be
how they function
to stretch the skin

how breasts grow high —
the beautiful brown tips.

When he sleeps
I sit in the bathroom
eating figs.

I imagine
this is what it looks like

when he puts his mouth
over me.

iii. The plumber

The flesh between bones and skin
has been there since the beginning

the nudity between a rib and a fig
hasn't changed shape —

but I've called in a plumber
to fix the hole underneath the kitchen sink.

He's working on leaks and taking peeks
and I very much think

so deep into the pink, somewhere between
his wrench and his screw,
he's sure to tickle something
to remind me of you.

iv. It could have been Eve, it could have been anyone

When they unearthed the bones
removed the dirt and put each one in place
they concluded that they were looking at a woman —
there it is, they said, *that's the rib she was built from.*

But then someone brought them a fig
and they saw for themselves, after it was split in two
that instead of a rib, woman is
built from a hole that holds her secrets like children.

Vinegar

… and for my thirst they gave me vinegar to drink.

— Psalm 69:21

She douches with vinegar to rid
her insides of the taste of iron.
She douches with vinegar, and she
douches with vinegar, with vinegar
to dissolve the claw she thinks is
still scraping away inside her.

And the pro-life movement is investing in
coat hangers now because the pro-life movement knows
the new legislation will do the job and skyrocket
the demand. The pro-life movement has its nose
on the pulse of what it is women need and the pro-life movement
will happily supply, crooked as crooked as witches' fingers
as they are, to help their cause.

I bet it was the same with nails
after Pontius Pilate let the crowd decide
which man to set free.

She douches with vinegar. And it stings.

The Body of Christ

The body of Christ is a tension of wires — a container for
the electric, a movement, the soul. The body of Christ is best
served up on a cross, arms outstretched and open for business.
The body of Christ is bankrupt because the body of Christ has
holes: wrist holes, side hole, eye holes, mouth hole, and an asshole,
amen. The body of Christ is resilient and full of cockroaches.
The body of Christ is a body in longing, its mouth open
wanting a kiss. The body of Christ is so much more than
John the Baptist's head on a platter: the body of Christ is
static skin stretched over the bones of the dead. The body of
Christ, the body of Christ, the body of Christ, amen. The body of Christ
is your body spread out on a bed, down to fuck. The body of Christ
is your cock hard as a nail. The body of Christ is you looking up at me,
trapped in ecstasy. The body of Christ shaking with joy and laughter;
the body of Christ covered in lambskin; the body of Christ,
the body of Christ, the body of Christ and I cum three times with
the body of Christ inside me. The body of Christ trembles like a
beetle, rides it out, goes soft, lies there belly up. The body of Christ
came out of a woman's hole and so it goes that the body of Christ is
divine. The body of Christ knows its way around a hammer.
The body of Christ is a taxidermist's fantasy, a pedophile's wet dream:
the body of Christ gets mounted over and over and no one gives a damn.
The body of Christ, the body of Christ, the body of Christ,
Κύριε ελέησον, the body of Christ. The body of Christ have mercy.
The body of Christ is crying. The body of Christ is dying, and yet,
the body of Christ refuses to die because the body of Christ is
full of cockroaches. The body of Christ needs a glass of water.
The body of Christ is a centrefold, hanging from the altar
and the body of Christ is topless and it's turning me on amen
and hallelujah. The body of Christ is some people's idea of a
good time. The body of Christ cut from its foreskin was the first
act of violence against the body of Christ. The body of Christ,
the body of Christ, the body of Christ sleeps with whores
and fishes. The body of Christ looks down at me, says *σώσε με*.
The body of Christ is a piece of bread going stale because the body
of Christ is the poster boy for decay. The body of Christ,

the body of Christ, the body of Christ is denied three times,
and the body of Christ is full of cockroaches, and the body of Christ
is just a body, and the body of Christ is starting to smell,
amen.

Like Oranges

She tells him it feels *like oranges*, the kind she used to pluck from
the trees in her father's village in Greece: vibrant
and round and full. In the bedroom his body clings to hers,
like Van Gogh's ear before the cut. On the wall next to the bed,
there's this photo of herself, her sisters and her two cousins,
standing in front of two orange trees in her aunt's yard.
The oranges are covered in snow (the only time she
or her sisters ever saw snow for all of the three years
that they lived there) and to look at that photo now, she knows
it's too old and blurry to tell anything from the faces of them
as children back then; still, she remembers it being joyful
and so she tells him, knowing herself to be as quiet as snow
that it feels *like oranges* when he touches her there.

They say Van Gogh painted his best oranges before he cut
bits of his ear off but her lover, well, he doesn't care about any
of that, or how important it is to be careful and delicate
with one's self in order to be careful and delicate with everything else.
It's two days later, and she's in his kitchen and he's offering up a jar,
tells her *me Ma, she makes the best marmalade.* She takes her knife,
digs into the open mouth and pulls out the orange guts of it: vibrant,
in slivers, sharp. And it tastes good. Afterwards, he picks up
his banjo (her lover has a banjo) and plucks at the strings;
as his fingers move it sounds *like oranges* and so he keeps plucking
and it's as if the banjo falls apart into oranges in his hands:
oranges tumbling, over and over until they fill the room.

And she tells him it's *like oranges* watching him go hard for her,
his cock as vibrant and full as a segment exposed from under
the orange rind of his foreskin. She knows to be delicate with him —
that to be soft and gentle with him, is to be soft and gentle with herself.
She thinks back to herself as a child, a piece of orange fruit in her hand,
and she knows there is nothing joyful in what Van Gogh did,
cutting himself like that; no, she does not believe her lover has to do
the same, offer her a piece of himself — not in a room where

his Ma's marmalade sits open on the kitchen table,
next to a knife with bits of orange still stuck to it.

Love is Stuck

L'amour est un oiseau rebelle.

— Habanera (aria), *Carmen*

Love stands poised on the inside of a coffee cup
un oiseau rebelle ready for take-off
as though all it would take to get into my mouth
is a head, cocked in my direction

In Defence of Lemons

What a difference, if lemons were the first offering:
the sharp taste of clean diving into every cell, the acid cry
of freedom and the vulva coming back from the dead —

and the vulva coming back, coming back a ribbon of yellow
tied 'round cock-bark and sex begins: the sharp taste
of clean diving into every cell, and it feels like fuck.

Honey

I thought you came from dirt
the kind that tasted of iron
and looked of red clay, mixed with
enough water to keep the blood moving
through your body at a constant pace.

Then it happened, and for all
that happened then, you were made
too little of water, too much like clay —
your blood was not blood; it had turned to mud instead.

But if your blood was not blood, if it had
stopped moving through your body
at a constant pace, then my body was not a body;
a glass jar full of honey had taken its place.

Go ask the bees, or the man who blew the glass
into shape — they will tell you there is an art to mercy
and for all that happened then, here is where it sticks:

I made sure to tell him to blow the glass thin,
just enough to break under your weight, cover you
in all I had to give.

I Do Not Think My Eyes are Pretty

but I
cannot find
a man
who will
agree with me

every one
who has seen them
considers them

quite capable
of turning things
to meat

they tell me

this makes them pretty
like a slaughterhouse

Sweet Morag

Ride my stallion Morag!

— Margaret Laurence, *The Diviners*

I love to watch you
undress. Like a flower
showing off in the sun,
you stretch yourself out

and there, lingering
beyond the petals
of your hands and feet,
a stamen to court bees.

But I am no queen
and that hum
between my legs
is no hive; it is
wilder than that.

My lily boy in heat
my sweet Morag
your body could lead
a horse to water

so ride me, ride me, ride me

Horse Logic

Yes, I love it, and I love it most of all. No point in being
dainty or delicate — no, not with something that's as deep
as a horse nostril, darker than a hole in a wall. I love it
the way an executioner loves the sound of a guillotine
but darling, just be careful where you put that head,
for it may have been that sound, as it chopped away
at the *tête* of Marie Antoinette, a sound so tight, so wet,
it turned half the world to *cunt!* as hers took its last breath.
And I love it, and the legend of teeth — a diagnosed condition
or a spiritual disease. I love it for the way it walks on land
like a fish out of water, its fish-mouth making the shape of an *O:*
O for the eye of Orwell, and O for the Organ, and O for the
Omicron and O for the Opening into the Underworld — and I love
the way you go to hell in it, and I love the way it spits you out
in spring, but come winter, I love the way it pulls you back in, and
O, O, O — I love it most of all for the way it makes your mother cry.
It's a god, an immortal beast; when it howls, it's something only dogs
can hear, and I love the way it turns itself into a dog for you: I love
the way it knows you have the kind of body a dog would lie down
next to. I love the way it bleeds out cherries — a gift-horse with a
mouthful of fruit, turning girls to women. I love the way you go
digging for a pit — even if it's a pit not worth planting — yes,
I love the way it knows something you don't. I love the way it feasts
on love, and I love the way it knows something you don't.
I love the way it eats meat down to the bone, and I love the way
it knows — I love the way it knows something you don't. I love it
for the way it competes and wins at death: hung like a noose
like a Tom Waits song, I love the way it breaks the neck
of your triumphant hard-on. When there's no bread left to eat
I love the way it says *Let them eat pussy instead!* I love it,
and I love it most of all: a horse's head, in your bed.

Bee's Wing

I

Pull the wing off a bee and it will still
die for the sting.

I think about the times I've pulled my feet
out of shoes too small to fit,
how many times
I tore the nail free from the toe
and I wonder

if this is dying for the sting for pulling off a bee's wing
until it hits me that a toenail is more like the myth
of a complete other thing with wings.

II

Skin breaks for being thin as a bee's wing
and as I feel your cock go soft, pull back,
it's clear you died a little death for the sting of it too.

Bodies spent, a myth
with wings stirs:

in the ash, death reigns fertile;
from the ash a bird rises —
from the ash, a new toenail begins.

The New Woman

Every man has the hands of his mother. You are no different.
Bring them here to me. Place them on my chest. Hold me.
My body is small and fat and it wants you. See how it opens.
My body is a small bird and it wants you. Hold me. Take me in
with your mother's hands. Show me what she taught you
of love and wanting. If you want me to beg for it, I will.
See how my body wants you. See how it opens and wants
you. Hold me. Keep me still. Take me with your mother's hands
and love me. Show me how your body comes to love.
I want you. If you want me to beg for it, I will. My body
is small, like a bird, and it wants you. I am a bird in your mother's
hands. Feel the delicate bones holding me together. Suck at the fat
of my longing. Hold me. Show me what to do with your body.
I want you. I am a bird and I want you. If you want me to beg for it,
I will. I am a bird that has landed into the open hands of your mother.
Hold me. Feel the beating of red muscle under my skin.
Run your palm along the delicate bones keeping me together.
I want you. See how my body wants you. Love me with
your mother's hands. Curl your bones around me. I am a small bird
in your hands. I want you. If you want me to beg for it, I will.
I am a small bird. I am a small bird with delicate bones.
You are the new woman. You have your mother's hands
and your body is the body of the new woman. Hold me.
If you want me to beg for it, I will. I want you. Curl your hands
around me. I want you. Show me how you've come to love.
I want you. I am a small bird that loves you. My body
grows fat and wet for you. Take me. Take me with your mother's
hands. Love me. If you want me to beg for it, I will.
I will throw myself against your body, ask for nothing; hope
for mercy. Every man has the hands of his mother.

Holes

There are holes in everything.
In the village where my mother grew up
there were holes in the speakers of the sound system
and that is how the women heard the alarm, knew
to hide their husbands in holes under the floorboards
when the Nazis came looking for men to kill.
They never found my grandfather because
my grandmother understood the nature of a hole:
a hole is built to hold things; it takes things in to keep them safe.
A hole is built around the O of love.

In 1986, the holes in those speakers spat out different sounds;
they were the sounds of Easter, and Jesus rising from the
dead — *Χριστός ανέστη εκ νεκρον* — and there were holes
in the lambs where the metal stakes were run through, their bodies
carried on shoulders — a sign of the cross — out onto the hot pits
in the streets. A pit is another word for a hole and I remember
those pits lined up, one after the other, coals burning
like the split-open guts of cigarettes.

Cigarette companies understand that the mouth is a hole, that it is
in the mouth's nature to want something to suck. Cigarettes
fill the void. A void is another word for a hole, and there were
voids in all those bodies turning on the spits, voids made by knives.
Those voids made me think of the crucifixion, the hole that was made
in Jesus' side to make sure he was dead. But everybody knows
you don't need to make a hole in something to check if it's dead.
A nose has holes and a nose can smell death and death smells of fat
and passion rendered down to ashes.

My grandmother was too big for death to render her
because my grandmother was too big for cancer. Cancer is not
another word for holes. Cancer is another word for infinity.
Infinity is what happens to a cell when apoptosis cannot be turned on,
and the cell does not know when to stop multiplying and will not die.

Repeat: cancer is not another word for holes, but my grandmother knew that the nature of holes can sometimes be as infinite as cancer.

Life is full of holes. And some holes are black. Black holes go on until infinity. Infinity is another word for forever. When the doctors took out my grandmother's tumour, they opened up a black hole in her breast that went on until forever. Forever tramples death — *θανάτω θάνατον πατήσας και τοις εν τοις μνήμασι ζωήν χαρισάμενος.* Forever is a hole built around the O of love. *Χριστός ανέστη! Christ is risen! Αληθώς ανέστη! Indeed He is risen!*

And so it goes that the body never dies; the body comes out of a hole built around the O of love and the O of love saved my grandfather because the Nazis never understood the nature of holes. They only understood the nature of efficiency and dug holes big enough and deep enough to hold many bodies.

Ovum

A woman is born with all the eggs she could ever possibly carry.
Periods, pills and prophylactics will foil most — but for those that
make it through, childbirth will turn her sex into a lion's mouth.
This is where the term pussy comes from.

Fucking for the first time is like a fried egg, sunny side up:
there's the foreplay of oil getting hot, the cracked shell oozing
a nakedness that is sexy because it is see-through. White spits and pops
in heat, gasping at the edges like fingers that clutch because
something good is coming. The yolk trembles. Don't break it.
Not yet.

A poached egg is a great swimmer; a scrambled egg kicks and has
a fit in the pan. A poached egg holds onto secrets like a cherry
or a blister, so long as you don't pop it; a scrambled egg spills
its guts out, cums all over itself. A poached egg isn't funny, prefers
to be alone; a scrambled egg digs a crowd, can tell a joke. A poached egg
will die young of unnatural causes; a scrambled egg fights death —
over time, it turns to rubber, feels like an old man.

Oh-Oh-Oh-vum! *Oh-Oh-Oh*-val! *Oh-Oh- Oh*-ver easy *oeuf*!
Oh-ver and *Oh*-ver, the egg came first.

If the world is an oyster, an egg is a universe unto itself,
with its own sun, its own galaxy — and even if the world is
an oyster, a string of pearls cannot compare to the beauty
of an egg boiled perfectly: touch it and it will yield, and yield,
like a testicle.

You Taste of Fish

Do not give your lover a fish.
Instead, teach them how. And so
the tongue worms, and your lover
becomes rod.

Salt

Love is a dog from hell.

— Charles Bukowski

I filled my mouth with words.
They sat on my tongue, waiting for you
to draw them out with your mouth,
the way the tide pulls on grains of sand.
I would have given them all to you
like sand, giving way to salt in every wave.

I told people that your smell
was like a bee: buzzing up one nostril
then flying into the other, as though my nose
were a flower in need of sex.
They were concerned with the amount of salt
in my diet: *it will lead to delirium* they said.

I made myself forget what you looked like —
your open mouth, your flirting hair — until I saw you again.
It gave my eyes a thrill to take in your measurements
and feast on a body so fit, as if for the first time.
For the thrill and from that thrill, I turned to salt:
another pillar, another Lot's wife.

I listened for the sounds of birds
so that I would come to know the difference
between songs of morning and songs of night
for the different times of day we were together.
I preserved the memory of the weight of your body
in grains of salt a thousand years old.

And there, as though I was underneath you still,
for the tide and the bee, for my eyes
and the sounds of birds in the morning,

the sounds of birds at night,
I confess that I laid myself down then
like a dog, for love.

Goya Knew Better

There are those who believe
woman is a loser, so the story goes,
yes, woman is a loser, straight from the apple core;
and for every story that makes it so
there is another about man
built with one bone missing, another bone sticking out —
even still, Goya knew the difference
between cocks and diviner rods, and for the way
the *maja desnuda* extended her body
like a fist unfurling, he knew better than to mistake
an open hand for surrender.

Your Hand Does Not Impress Me as Much

It is like a forest or the start of a parade; don't ask me to decide —
some days, I want it to be both.

Where other women might peck, be satisfied
with the seeds and worms that have settled into the
basket of your hand; your hand does not impress me as much
as the little fist of hair that comes punching up through
your shirt collar. Here, the animal above
and the animal underneath are two parts of the
same fruit, split for the taking; for a second, I am reminded
of a story about a snake that came out on a day
a woman needed a little convincing. But oh, my desire,
made of arms and hands and teeth, it knows how to reach out,
knows how to grab, how to bite, all on its own.

All on its own, your hand does not impress me as much as mine:
each finger a jackal and a lion for a thumb — they sprawl
across your body, plotting for your throat.

Maggot Fingers

He doesn't realise he's going to die one day,
doesn't realise he comes from dead people.
He thinks he is made of stronger stuff than flesh,
dips his maggot fingers into the pit of my body
and calls it forever.

He thinks my body is where love goes to die
to come alive again.

He declares his love, says my heart is as stubborn
as a cockroach; my tongue, a swollen beehive gone mad.
He loves to think of us as insects dancing on the table
of death's banquet, our bodies tearing, and tearing through
like the birth of the new man.

One day, his fingers will turn to flies; my body,
more vinegar than honey.

Flies

I

The dark pupil of the eye
is a fly pressed against glass

legs as thin as lashes
and wings like the lens of a camera
that sees right through
to where two bodies hang
in heat, covered in bullets.

Here, the eyes adjust
to the darkness in every hole.

II

Love's stare
is a sunburn
through a magnifying glass
and it peels skin off in
bits thin as hymens and eyelids.
Here, the distance
between the moist
and the macabre

is the same
as the distance
between Mussolini
and his mistress
hanging from meat hooks:

the lens of a camera
captures two bodies
deep in the sockets
of an underworld
where only flies
have eyes.

Madrid is a Woman

He thinks I am only forty percent right; for what it's worth,
he isn't a woman — for him, it's hard. Half-way through our
second glass of sangria, he takes my hand, touches it
as though he's been around hands all his life.

We talk of love and Lorca's *duende* — the dirt of feeling,
the darkness in the fight. He says the fat in my palm
makes me a very sensual woman. Like this city, I say,
these hands mark where a body begins and ends; they wave a
circle around my borders and make a sign —
here, the entrance to Madrid.

Where love is of the body love has no grounds to be outside
the only place with the space to feel it. Still touching my hand —
if he keeps at it, he might not let it go — he says I have a very
sexual view of love; for what it's worth I think
he is only forty percent right.

Love Bares the Wood

His body was pulled from the cross
and turned into bread for all eternity —
passed, like love, from one body into another
as if the only way to feel love is to eat love.

But love is not a food. And that feeling of fullness
isn't what it feels like to love someone.

The first time my grandmother ate ice cream on a stick
she loved it so much, she wanted my grandfather to try it —
she loved him so much, she wanted him to know
what eating something for the first time would taste like,
the complete newness of it. So she bought one
and put it in her purse, for when she would see him again.

But it melted into a sea of white cream, leaving the stick
as the offering, the only solid thing pulled out
from the deep cave of her purse.

Now, you can go ahead and tell me that I'm wrong
to deny the power of bread, wrong to compare
the body of Christ to a pool of melted ice cream, but

I know love

and love does not compare suffering;
love bares the wood.

The Bees

Tell me how you laid your body down
and summoned all the bees to come —
how they landed on your chest, your
thighs and feet, how they shook and
danced there, and the line blurred
between the offerings.

Tell me how your wild heart grew wilder
at the feel of staple-thin legs entwined
in your pubic hair, at the sight of the one
solitary bee breaking free to perch
at the tip of your cock, and there, again,
how the line blurred once more
between the offerings.

Tell me how the flowers of your eyes
are no match for orchids or white lilies,
that your eyes are the new flowers of death;
the bees, the shroud. Tell me how you felt
each sting, then let them crawl into your mouth
to die, and I will tell you every bee is me
and we will watch the line blur, for the last time,
between the offerings.

ABOUT THE AUTHOR

DIMITRA XIDOUS is originally from Ottawa, Canada. Her poems have been published in literary journals in Canada, Ireland and the US, including *Room*, *Penduline* and *Colony*. The featured poet in the Spring 2014 issue of *The Stinging Fly*, Dimitra's work was included in the anthology *New Planet Cabaret* (New Island, 2013). She was a finalist in the 2014 *Malahat Review* Open Season Awards, shortlisted for both the Bridport Prize (2013) and for the Over the Edge Emerging New Writer Award (2013), and long-listed for the Montreal International Poetry Competition (2011). She curates The Ash Sessions, a poetry and music showcase at Nick's Coffee Company, Ranelagh, Dublin. Along with Patrick Chapman, Dimitra co-founded and co-edits *The Pickled Body* (www.thepickledbody.com), a quarterly poetry and art magazine. She lives in Dublin.

Visit her website at www.dimitraxidous.com

ABOUT THE ARTIST

RIA CZERNIAK is a visual artist and musician from Dublin. She has created and exhibited work in a variety of media ranging from etching and drawing to textiles and installation. In October 2012, she released her debut album entitled *Souvenir*, for which she created all the art work. The album was warmly received in *Hot Press*, which called it 'One not to be missed'. Ria also illustrated the inaugural publication of *The Pickled Body* poetry quarterly in 2013. In both her visual art and songwriting, Ria Czerniak has a distinctive style, combining an enduring commitment to storytelling with her painstaking attention to detail.

Contact her at riaczerniak@gmail.com.

NOTES

Epigraph — taken from Federico García Lorca's *Blood Wedding* (1932).

Animals — The epigraph is taken from Marty McConnell's poem 'Frida Kahlo to Marty McConnell'.

Hello Dalí — The epigragh is taken from a quote by Salvador Dalí. The painting being referenced in the poem is *Geopoliticus Child Watching the Birth of the New Man* (1943).

You Cannot Tell Me — The epigraph is taken from a quote by Federico García Lorca.

Six Pack — A *torcedor* is a Cuban cigar maker.

Death is Always Inevitable — The line, 'It was inevitable' is the opening to the novel *Love in the Time of Cholera* by Gabriel García Márquez (Alfred A. Knopf, 1984).

Vinegar — The epigraph is taken from Psalm 69:21 — 'Instead, they gave me gall for my food, and for my thirst they gave me vinegar to drink' (Holman Christian Standard Bible).

The Body of Christ — Κύριε ελέησον means 'Lord, have mercy'; σώσε με means 'save me'.

Love is Stuck — The epigraph is taken from the aria 'Habanera' from the opera *Carmen* by Georges Bizet. The epigraph translates as follows: Love is a rebellious bird.

Sweet Morag — The epigraph is from the novel *The Diviners* by Margaret Laurence (Virago, 2008).

Holes — The translation of the Greek lines in the poem are taken from Christos Anesti, Greek Easter Hymn, and translates as follows: Christ is risen from the dead, trampling down death by death, and to those in the tombs, granting life.

Salt — The epigraph is taken from Charles Bukowski's *Love is a Dog from Hell* (Black Sparrow Press, 1977).